The Art of Needle Tatting

A Comprehensive Guide to Mastering the Craft

Delicia Stone

Table of Content

CHAPTER 1

Needle tatting is a technique used to create delicate lace-like designs using a small, handheld needle instead of a traditional tatting shuttle. It's a form of lace-making that involves the manipulation of thread to form knots and loops, resulting in intricate patterns and designs. Needle tatting is often preferred by beginners or those who find it challenging to manipulate a shuttle, as it requires less dexterity and coordination.

In needle tatting, the needle is used to form the knots and loops directly onto the thread, allowing for greater control and precision in the creation of the desired design. This technique typically involves making a series of double stitches (ds), picots (small loops), and rings, which are then joined together to form chains and more complex motifs.

One of the advantages of needle tatting is its versatility. It can be used to create a wide range of items, including jewelry, accessories, home décor, and embellishments for clothing and textiles. With practice and creativity, needle tatters can produce intricate lace patterns that rival the beauty of traditional shuttle tatting.

Overall, needle tatting offers a rewarding and enjoyable way to express creativity while producing timeless pieces of handmade lace.

History and Origins

The history and origins of needle tatting are intertwined with the broader history of tatting itself, which dates back centuries and has roots in various cultures around the world. Tatting, in its traditional form using a shuttle, has been practiced for generations as a way to create delicate lacework by knotting and looping threads together.

The exact origins of tatting are somewhat obscure, as the craft likely developed independently in different regions over time. However, some historical evidence suggests that tatting may have originated in Europe during the 17th or 18th centuries, possibly as a form of decorative lace-making practiced by aristocrats and wealthy individuals.

Needle tatting, specifically, emerged later as an alternative method to shuttle tatting. While shuttle tatting was the predominant technique for centuries, needle tatting gained popularity in the 20th century, particularly in the mid-20th century when needles designed specifically for tatting became more widely available.

The development of needle tatting needles, which are slender with a small hook at one end, made it easier for crafters to create tatting designs without the need for a traditional shuttle. This innovation opened up tatting to a wider audience, including those who found shuttle tatting too challenging or cumbersome.

Throughout the 20th century, needle tatting continued to evolve, with tatters experimenting with new techniques, materials, and designs. Today, needle tatting remains a popular craft practiced by individuals around the world, celebrated for its beauty, versatility, and intricate designs.

While the exact timeline and origins of needle tatting may be difficult to pinpoint, its development and evolution reflect the enduring appeal of tatting as a timeless art form cherished by generations of crafters.

Benefits and Versatility of Needle Tatting

Needle tatting offers a multitude of benefits and boasts remarkable versatility, making it a beloved craft for enthusiasts worldwide.

Accessibility: One of the primary benefits of needle tatting is its accessibility. Unlike shuttle tatting, which requires mastering the technique of manipulating a shuttle, needle tatting can be easier for beginners to learn. The use of a needle allows for greater control and precision, making it an ideal choice for those new to tatting or those who find shuttle tatting challenging.

Portability: Needle tatting is highly portable, requiring only a small needle and a ball of thread or yarn. This makes it a perfect craft for on-the-go creativity. Whether you're traveling, commuting, or simply relaxing at home, needle tatting allows you to indulge your creative impulses wherever you are.

Versatility in Materials: Needle tatting is incredibly versatile in terms of the materials that can be used. While traditional tatting is typically done with fine cotton thread, needle tatters can experiment with a wide range of threads, yarns, and even wire. This versatility opens up endless possibilities for creativity and allows tatters to explore different textures, colors, and effects in their work.

Adaptability in Design: Needle tatting offers flexibility and adaptability in design, allowing tatters to create a wide variety of projects, from intricate lace doilies to delicate jewelry and beyond. With needle tatting, you can easily customize designs, incorporate beads or other embellishments, and experiment with different stitches and techniques to achieve the desired look.

Time Efficiency: While tatting, in general, is known for its time-intensive nature, needle tatting can be more time-efficient compared to shuttle tatting, especially for certain projects or techniques. The use of a needle can streamline the tatting process and eliminate the need for winding and unwinding thread from a shuttle, saving time and effort.

Therapeutic Benefits: Like many forms of needlework, needle tatting can have therapeutic benefits for practitioners. The repetitive motions involved in tatting can be calming and meditative, providing a sense of relaxation and stress relief. Additionally, the satisfaction of creating something beautiful with one's own hands can boost mood and overall well-being.

Community and Connection: Needle tatting enthusiasts often find camaraderie and support within the tatting community. Whether through in-person workshops, online forums, or social media groups, tatters can connect with fellow enthusiasts, share tips and techniques, and find inspiration in each other's work.

Overall, needle tatting offers a wealth of benefits, from its accessibility and versatility to its therapeutic qualities and sense of community. Whether you're a seasoned tatter or just beginning your tatting journey, needle tatting is sure to captivate and inspire you with its endless possibilities.

Essential Tools and Materials

To embark on your needle tatting journey, you'll need a few essential tools and materials to get started.

Tatting Needle: The heart of needle tatting is, of course, the tatting needle itself. These needles are specifically designed for tatting and have a small hook at one end to facilitate the creation of knots and loops. Tatting needles come in various sizes, so it's helpful to have a few different sizes on hand to accommodate different thread weights and project requirements.

Thread or Yarn: Choose a thread or yarn suitable for needle tatting. Traditionally, tatting is done with fine cotton thread, but you can experiment with other materials such as silk, polyester, or even metallic threads for different effects. Consider the weight and texture of the thread when selecting materials for your project.

Scissors: A good pair of sharp scissors is essential for cutting your thread as you work. Choose scissors with fine, pointed blades for precision cutting.

Beads and Embellishments (optional): If you'd like to add extra flair to your tatting projects, consider incorporating beads or other embellishments. Beads can be threaded onto your tatting thread and worked into your design as desired. Experiment with different bead sizes, shapes, and colors to achieve unique effects.

Pattern or Design Guide: Having a pattern or design guide is helpful, especially for beginners. Look for needle tatting books, online tutorials, or printable patterns to follow along with as you practice and learn new techniques. As you gain experience, you may feel confident enough to design your own patterns.

Tatting Shuttle (optional): While not strictly necessary for needle tatting, some tatters find it helpful to have a tatting shuttle on hand for certain techniques or to wind thread onto for storage. Shuttles can also be used to hold additional lengths of thread if you're working on a particularly large project.

Thimble (optional): If you find yourself pushing the needle through tight stitches, a thimble can help protect your finger and provide additional leverage. Choose a thimble that fits comfortably and allows you to maneuver the needle with ease.

Storage Container: Keep your tatting needles, thread, and other supplies organized and accessible by storing them in a dedicated container or case. This will help prevent tangling and loss of materials and make it easier to transport your supplies when you're tatting on the go.

With these essential tools and materials in hand, you'll be well-equipped to dive into the world of needle tatting and start creating beautiful lace designs and intricate motifs with ease.

CHAPTER 2

Basic Techniques
Making Double Stitches (ds):

Double stitches (ds) are the fundamental building blocks of tatting. They form the basis of most tatting patterns and are used to create chains, rings, and other elements.

Step 1: Thread your tatting needle with the desired length of thread. Leave a tail of about 6 inches for later use.

Step 2: Hold the needle in your dominant hand and grasp the working thread between your thumb and index finger.

Step 3: Insert the needle through the loop formed by your fingers from top to bottom, catching the working thread on the hook of the needle.

Step 4: Pull the needle and working thread through the loop to form a small loop or knot on the needle.

Step 5: Tighten the loop by gently pulling the working thread. This completes one double stitch (ds).

Step 6: Repeat steps 3-5 to create additional double stitches as needed for your pattern.

Creating Picots:

Picots are small loops formed between stitches in tatting. They are used for decorative purposes and to create spacing between elements in a tatting pattern.

Step 1: After completing a double stitch (ds), bring the needle and thread to the desired position for the picot.

Step 2: Hold the thread taut and use your non-dominant hand to create a small loop by wrapping the thread around your index finger or a picot gauge. The size of the loop will determine the size of the picot.

Step 3: Insert the needle through the loop from top to bottom, catching the loop on the hook of the needle.

Step 4: Pull the needle and thread through the loop to form the picot.

Step 5: Tighten the picot by gently pulling the working thread. The picot should be snug but not too tight to allow movement.

Step 6: Continue tatting according to your pattern, incorporating picots as needed for decoration or spacing.

Forming Rings:

Rings are circular elements in tatting that are created by joining double stitches (ds) together in a continuous loop.

Step 1: Begin by making a small loop with the working thread, leaving a tail of about 6 inches for later use.

Step 2: Insert the needle through the loop from top to bottom, catching the loop on the hook of the needle.

Step 3: Pull the needle and thread through the loop to form the first double stitch (ds) of the ring.

Step 4: Continue making double stitches (ds) by inserting the needle through the previous double stitch and pulling the thread through to form new stitches. The number of stitches will depend on your pattern.

Step 5: Once you've completed the desired number of stitches, bring the needle and thread back through the first double stitch to close the ring.

Step 6: Tighten the ring by gently pulling on the tail and working thread until the stitches are snug and the ring is closed securely.

Step 7: Continue tatting according to your pattern, incorporating rings as needed for the desired design.

Joining Picots:

Joining picots allows you to connect different tatting elements together, such as rings and chains, to create intricate designs.

Step 1: Begin by completing a ring or chain that has picots where you want to make the joins.

Step 2: Bring the needle and thread to the position where you want to join the picot.

Step 3: Insert the needle through the picot of the previous element from top to bottom, catching the picot on the hook of the needle.

Step 4: Pull the needle and thread through the picot to form a loop around it.

Step 5: Continue tatting according to your pattern, incorporating the joined picots as needed to connect elements together.

Step 6: Tighten the join by gently pulling on the working thread until the stitches are snug and the elements are securely connected.

Forming Chains:

Chains are linear elements in tatting that are created by joining double stitches (ds) together in a continuous line.

Step 1: Begin by making a small loop with the working thread, leaving a tail of about 6 inches for later use.

Step 2: Insert the needle through the loop from top to bottom, catching the loop on the hook of the needle.

Step 3: Pull the needle and thread through the loop to form the first double stitch (ds) of the chain.

Step 4: Continue making double stitches (ds) by inserting the needle through the previous double stitch and pulling the thread through to form new stitches.

Step 5: Once you've completed the desired length of the chain, secure it by making a small picot or by joining it to another element using the joining picot technique described above.

Step 6: Tighten the chain by gently pulling on the tail and working thread until the stitches are snug and the chain is straight and secure.

Step 7: Continue tatting according to your pattern, incorporating chains as needed for the desired design.

Advanced Technique
Split Rings:

Split rings allow for more intricate and decorative tatting designs by creating sections within a ring that can be worked separately.

Step 1: Begin by making a loop with the working thread and completing the first half of the split ring by forming double stitches (ds) as usual.

Step 2: Before closing the ring completely, leave a small loop of thread at the desired point where the split will occur.

Step 3: Insert the needle through the loop of thread, creating the split, and continue tatting the second half of the ring by forming additional double stitches (ds).

Step 4: Once the second half of the ring is complete, close the ring by bringing the needle and thread back through the initial double stitch.

Step 5: Tighten the split ring by gently pulling on the working thread until the stitches are snug and the ring is securely closed.

Step 6: Continue tatting according to your pattern, incorporating split rings as needed for the desired design.

Cluny Tatting:

Cluny tatting is a technique used to create long, narrow strips of fabric or lace resembling leaves or petals.

Step 1: Begin by wrapping the working thread around a narrow, pointed object such as a cluny shuttle or a specially designed cluny hook.

Step 2: Insert the needle through the wrapped thread to form the base of the cluny leaf.

Step 3: Bring the needle back through the loop created by the wrapped thread and pull it tight to secure.

Step 4: Use the needle to make a series of double stitches (ds) around the wrapped thread, forming the shape of the cluny leaf.

Step 5: Once the desired number of stitches is reached, secure the end of the leaf by passing the needle through the base of the stitches and pulling it tight.

Step 6: Repeat the process to create additional cluny leaves as needed for your pattern.

Step 7: Incorporate the cluny leaves into your tatting design by joining them to chains, rings, or other elements using the joining picot technique or by attaching them directly with a needle.

Adding Color Variations:

Adding color variations to your tatting projects can enhance their visual appeal and create unique, eye-catching designs.

Step 1: Begin by selecting the colors of thread you want to use for your project. You can use a single color for a uniform look or multiple colors for a more vibrant effect.

Step 2: Tat the first section of your design using one color of thread, following the pattern instructions as usual.

Step 3: When you reach a point where you want to change colors, cut the working thread of the first color, leaving a tail of a few inches.

Step 4: Thread the needle with the second color of thread and continue tatting the next section of your design, joining it to the previous section using the joining picot technique.

Step 5: Repeat the process as needed to incorporate additional color changes throughout your tatting project, following the pattern instructions and joining sections together as you go.

Step 6: Once the project is complete, weave in any loose ends and secure them with a small knot or dab of fabric glue to prevent unraveling.

Adding Beads:

Incorporating beads into your tatting projects adds texture, sparkle, and dimension to your designs.

Step 1: Thread the desired number of beads onto your tatting thread before beginning your project. You can thread beads onto the entire length of thread or add them individually as you tat.

Step 2: Begin tatting your project as usual, making double stitches (ds) or forming rings and chains according to your pattern.

Step 3: When you reach a point where you want to add a bead, slide a bead down the thread until it rests against the last double stitch (ds) or picot.

Step 4: Continue tatting as usual, trapping the bead in place between stitches. You can incorporate beads into rings, chains, or picots as desired, adjusting the placement and number of beads to achieve the desired effect.

Step 5: Once the bead is in place, continue tatting according to your pattern, incorporating additional beads as needed.

Step 6: To secure the beads in place, you can make a small picot or loop around each bead, trapping it between stitches and preventing it from sliding along the thread.

Creating Mock Picots:

Mock picots are decorative elements created by folding and manipulating the thread to resemble traditional picots without actually forming knots.

Step 1: Begin tatting your project as usual, making double stitches (ds) or forming rings and chains according to your pattern.

Step 2: When you reach a point where you want to create a mock picot, fold the working thread back on itself to form a small loop or fold.

Step 3: Hold the loop or fold in place with your non-dominant hand while you continue tatting with your dominant hand.

Step 4: Continue tatting as usual, incorporating the mock picot into your pattern. You can join chains or rings to the mock picot using the joining picot technique, or you can simply leave it as a decorative element.

Step 5: Once the mock picot is in place, continue tatting according to your pattern, incorporating additional mock picots as needed.

Step 6: To secure the mock picots in place, you can make small stitches or loops around them, anchoring them to the adjacent stitches and preventing them from unraveling.

CHAPTER 3
Beginner Projects

Simple Tatting Bookmark

Materials Needed:

- Tatting needle
- Tatting thread
- Scissors

Instructions:

Begin by threading your tatting needle with the desired length of thread.

Start tatting by creating a ring with a few double stitches (ds), followed by a series of picots for decoration.

After completing the ring, continue tatting a chain of double stitches (ds) to form the length of the bookmark.

At the end of the chain, close with another ring, mirroring the first ring design.

Once you've completed the desired length of the bookmark, Cut off any extra thread and firmly secure the ends.

Optionally, add a tassel or decorative bead to the end of the bookmark for extra flair.

Miniature Tatting Earrings

Materials Needed:

- Tatting needle

- Tatting thread
- Earring hooks
- Scissors

Instructions:

Begin by tatting two small rings, each with a few double stitches (ds) and picots for decoration.

Next, tat a chain of double stitches (ds) to connect the two rings and form the loop for the earring hook.

Once the chain is complete, close with another small ring, mirroring the design of the first rings.

After completing both earrings, attach the earring hooks to the loops formed by the chains.

Cut off any extra thread and firmly secure the ends.

Optionally, add beads or embellishments to the earrings for extra sparkle.

Tatting Coaster

Materials Needed:

- Tatting needle
- Tatting thread
- Scissors

Instructions:

Begin by tatting a large ring to serve as the center of the coaster, using a combination of double stitches (ds) and picots for decoration.

After completing the central ring, tat a series of chains around the edge of the ring to form the body of the coaster.

Continue tatting additional rounds of chains, increasing the number of chains in each round to create a scalloped edge.

Once you've reached the desired size for the coaster, finish with a final round of picots or decorative stitches.

Cut off any extra thread and firmly secure the ends.

Optionally, block the coaster by dampening it slightly and pinning it into shape to dry, ensuring a flat and uniform appearance.

Simple Tatting Pendant

Materials Needed:

- Tatting needle
- Tatting thread
- Small pendant bail or jump ring
- Chain or cord for necklace
- Scissors

Instructions:

Start by tatting a small ring with a few double stitches (ds) and picots for decoration.

After completing the ring, tat a chain of double stitches (ds) to form the length of the pendant.

Once you've reached the desired length, close with another small ring, mirroring the design of the first ring.

Cut off any extra thread and firmly secure the ends.

Attach the pendant bail or jump ring to the top of the pendant using a small length of thread.

Thread the chain or cord through the bail or jump ring to complete the necklace.

Optionally, add beads or embellishments to the pendant for extra detail and sparkle.

Tatting Lace Coasters

Materials Needed:

- Tatting needle
- Tatting thread
- Coaster mold (optional)
- Fabric stiffener (optional)
- Scissors

Instructions:

Begin by tatting a small ring with a few double stitches (ds) and picots for decoration.

After completing the ring, tat a chain of double stitches (ds) to form the first round of the coaster.

Continue tatting additional rounds of chains, increasing the number of chains in each round to create a scalloped edge.

Once you've reached the desired size for the coaster, finish with a final round of picots or decorative stitches.

Cut off any extra thread and firmly secure the ends.

Optionally, block the coaster by dampening it slightly and pinning it into shape to dry, ensuring a flat and uniform appearance.

For added durability, you can stiffen the coaster by soaking it in fabric stiffener and allowing it to dry according to the manufacturer's instructions.

Once dry, your lace coasters are ready to use or display!

Tatting Keychain

Materials Needed:

- Tatting needle
- Tatting thread
- Keychain ring
- Scissors

Instructions:

Begin by tatting a small ring with a few double stitches (ds) and picots for decoration.

After completing the ring, tat a chain of double stitches (ds) to form the length of the keychain.

Once you've reached the desired length, close with another small ring, mirroring the design of the first ring.

Cut off any extra thread and firmly secure the ends.

Attach the keychain ring to the top of the tatting using a small length of thread.

Optionally, add beads or embellishments to the keychain for extra detail and charm.

Your tatting keychain is now ready to use or give as a handmade gift!

Tatting Lace Appliqué

Materials Needed:

- Tatting needle
- Tatting thread
- Fabric for appliqué base
- Fabric glue or needle and thread
- Scissors

Instructions:

Begin by tatting a small motif, such as a flower or leaf, using a combination of rings, chains, and picots.

Once the motif is complete, Cut off any extra thread and firmly secure the ends.

Prepare the fabric base for the appliqué by cutting it to the desired shape and size.

Attach the tatting motif to the fabric base using fabric glue or by stitching it in place with needle and thread.

Allow the glue to dry completely or finish securing the motif with additional stitching.

Once the appliqué is securely attached, trim any excess fabric from around the edges.

Your tatting lace appliqué can now be used to embellish clothing, accessories, home decor items, and more!

Tatting Lace Earrings

Materials Needed:

- Tatting needle
- Tatting thread
- Earring hooks
- Jump rings (optional)
- Beads or charms (optional)
- Scissors

Instructions:

Begin by tatting a small motif, such as a flower, heart, or simple geometric shape, using a combination of rings, chains, and picots.

Once the motif is complete, Cut off any extra thread and firmly secure the ends.

Prepare the earring hooks by attaching jump rings to the loop at the bottom (if they don't already have one attached).

Attach the tatting motif to the earring hooks using jump rings or by threading the loop of the motif directly onto the earring hooks.

If desired, add beads or charms to the earrings for extra embellishment and sparkle.

Once the earrings are assembled, adjust the positioning of the tatting motif and beads as needed.

Repeat the process to create a matching pair of earrings.

Your tatting lace earrings are now ready to wear or give as a handmade gift!

CHAPTER 4
Intermediate Projects

Tatting Lace Bookmark with Tassel

Materials Needed:

- Tatting needle
- Tatting thread
- Small bead for tassel (optional)
- Scissors

Instructions:

Tat a decorative motif, such as a flower or butterfly, using a combination of rings, chains, and picots.

Once the motif is complete, tat a chain for the length of the bookmark.

At the end of the chain, create another motif or a series of picots for decoration.

Optionally, add a tassel to the end of the bookmark by threading a small bead onto the working thread and tying a knot to secure it.

Cut the tassel ends to the preferred length.

Once the tatting is complete, weave in any loose ends and trim any excess thread.

Your tatting lace bookmark with a tassel is now ready to use or give as a handmade gift!

Tatting Lace Doily

Materials Needed:

- Tatting needle
- Tatting thread
- Doily pattern (available online or in tatting books)
- Fabric stiffener (optional)
- Blocking board or surface (optional)
- Pins (optional)
- Scissors

Instructions:

Select a doily pattern that matches your skill level and desired size.

Follow the pattern instructions to tat the doily, working rows of rings, chains, and picots as indicated.

Once the tatting is complete, weave in any loose ends and trim any excess thread.

Optionally, block the doily by dampening it slightly with water or fabric stiffener and pinning it into shape on a blocking board or surface.

Ensure the doily is fully dry before taking out the pins.

Your tatting lace doily is now ready to use as a decorative accent for tables, dressers, or other surfaces!

Tatting Lace Necklace

Materials Needed:

- Tatting needle
- Tatting thread
- Necklace chain or cord
- Jump rings
- Lobster clasp
- Beads or charms for embellishment (optional)
- Scissors

Instructions:

Tat a series of motifs, such as flowers, leaves, or geometric shapes, using a combination of rings, chains, and picots.

Once the motifs are complete, attach them to a necklace chain or cord using jump rings.

Arrange the motifs on the chain or cord in a pleasing arrangement, spacing them evenly along the length.

Optionally, add beads or charms between the motifs for extra embellishment.

Attach a lobster clasp to one end of the necklace chain or cord to fasten the necklace securely.

Your tatting lace necklace is now ready to wear and enjoy as a stylish and unique accessory!

Tatting Lace Coasters with Embellishments

Materials Needed:

- Tatting needle
- Tatting thread
- Coaster mold (optional)
- Fabric stiffener (optional)
- Beads, sequins, or charms for embellishment
- Fabric glue or needle and thread
- Scissors

Instructions:

Tat a set of lace coasters using a combination of rings, chains, and picots.

Once the tatting is complete, optionally block the coasters by dampening them slightly with fabric stiffener and pinning them into shape on a blocking board or surface.

Allow the coasters to dry completely before removing the pins.

Embellish the coasters with beads, sequins, or charms by attaching them to the tatting using fabric glue or by stitching them in place with needle and thread.

Once the embellishments are securely attached, trim any excess thread and weave in any loose ends.

Your tatting lace coasters with embellishments are now ready to use as elegant accents for your table settings or as thoughtful gifts for loved ones!

Tatting Lace Sachet with Lavender

Materials Needed:

- Tatting needle
- Tatting thread
- Fabric for sachet pouch
- Dried lavender buds or other potpourri
- Ribbon for tying
- Scissors

Instructions:

Tat a small lace motif, such as a flower or heart, to serve as the embellishment for your sachet.

Once the motif is complete, set it aside and prepare the fabric for the sachet pouch by cutting it to the desired size and shape.

Fold the fabric in half with the right sides together and stitch along the edges, leaving a small opening for filling.

Fill the sachet pouch with dried lavender buds or other potpourri, taking care not to overfill.

Insert the tatting lace motif into the opening of the sachet pouch and stitch it closed securely.

Finish the sachet by tying a ribbon around the top to secure it closed and add a decorative touch.

Your tatting lace sachet with lavender is now ready to use as a fragrant and decorative accent for your drawers, closets, or living spaces!

Tatting Lace Hair Clip

Materials Needed:

- Tatting needle
- Tatting thread
- Metal hair clip or barrette
- Fabric glue or needle and thread
- Scissors

Instructions:

Tat a small lace motif, such as a butterfly or flower, using a combination of rings, chains, and picots.

Once the motif is complete, Cut off any extra thread and firmly secure the ends.

Attach the tatting lace motif to a metal hair clip or barrette using fabric glue or by stitching it in place with needle and thread.

Allow the glue to dry completely or finish securing the motif with additional stitching.

Optionally, embellish the hair clip with beads, sequins, or charms for extra sparkle and flair.

Your tatting lace hair clip is now ready to wear as a stylish and unique accessory!

CHAPTER 5
Advanced Projects

Tatting Lace Doily with Raised Embroidery

Materials Needed:

- Tatting needle
- Tatting thread
- Doily pattern (available online or in tatting books)
- Fabric for doily base
- Embroidery thread or fine yarn
- Embroidery needle
- Fabric stiffener (optional)
- Blocking board or surface (optional)
- Pins (optional)
- Scissors

Instructions:

Select a doily pattern that incorporates advanced tatting techniques, such as split rings or cluny tatting.

Tat the doily according to the pattern instructions, working rows of rings, chains, and picots as indicated.

Once the tatting is complete, optionally block the doily by dampening it slightly with water or fabric stiffener and pinning it into shape on a blocking board or surface.

Ensure the doily is fully dry before taking out the pins.

Using embroidery thread or fine yarn, add raised embroidery to the surface of the doily, working over the tatting stitches to create intricate designs and textures.

Once the embroidery is complete, weave in any loose ends and trim any excess thread.

Your tatting lace doily with raised embroidery is now ready to use as a beautiful and unique accent for your home decor!

Tatting Lace Shawl or Wrap

Materials Needed:

- Tatting needle
- Tatting thread
- Shawl or wrap pattern (available online or in tatting books)
- Blocking board or surface
- Pins
- Fabric stiffener (optional)
- Ribbon or fringe for embellishment (optional)
- Scissors

Instructions:

Choose a shawl or wrap pattern that incorporates advanced tatting techniques, such as large motifs, intricate edging, or multiple rounds of tatting.

Tat the shawl or wrap according to the pattern instructions, working rows of rings, chains, and picots as indicated.

Once the tatting is complete, block the shawl or wrap by dampening it slightly with water or fabric stiffener and pinning it into shape on a blocking board or surface.

Allow the shawl or wrap to dry completely before removing the pins.

Optionally, add embellishments such as ribbon or fringe to the edges of the shawl or wrap for extra flair and elegance.

Your tatting lace shawl or wrap is now ready to wear as a stunning and sophisticated accessory for special occasions or everyday wear!

Tatting Lace Wedding Veil

Materials Needed:

- Tatting needle
- Tatting thread
- Wedding veil pattern (available online or in tatting books)
- Tulle fabric for veil base
- Comb or hairpin for attaching veil
- Fabric stiffener (optional)
- Blocking board or surface
- Pins
- Scissors

Instructions:

Select a wedding veil pattern that features intricate lace motifs and edging, such as roses, hearts, or snowflakes.

Tat the lace motifs and edging according to the pattern instructions, working rows of rings, chains, and picots as indicated.

Once the tatting is complete, block the lace motifs and edging by dampening them slightly with water or fabric stiffener and pinning them into shape on a blocking board or surface.

Allow the lace motifs and edging to dry completely before removing the pins.

Cut a piece of tulle fabric to the desired size and shape for the veil base, ensuring it is large enough to accommodate the tatting lace motifs and edging.

Attach the tatting lace motifs and edging to the tulle fabric using fabric glue or by stitching them in place with needle and thread.

Attach a comb or hairpin to the top edge of the veil for securing it to the bride's hair.

Optionally, add additional embellishments such as pearls, crystals, or sequins to the veil for extra sparkle and elegance.

Your tatting lace wedding veil is now ready to be worn as a breathtaking and timeless accessory for the bride on her special day!

Tatting Lace Table Runner

Materials Needed:

- Tatting needle
- Tatting thread
- Table runner pattern (available online or in tatting books)
- Fabric for table runner base
- Fabric stiffener (optional)
- Blocking board or surface
- Pins
- Scissors

Instructions:

Choose a table runner pattern that showcases advanced tatting techniques, such as large motifs, intricate edging, or multiple rounds of tatting.

Tat the table runner according to the pattern instructions, working rows of rings, chains, and picots as indicated.

Once the tatting is complete, block the table runner by dampening it slightly with water or fabric stiffener and pinning it into shape on a blocking board or surface.

Allow the table runner to dry completely before removing the pins.

Cut a piece of fabric to the desired size and shape for the table runner base, ensuring it is large enough to accommodate the tatting.

Attach the tatting to the fabric base using fabric glue or by stitching it in place with needle and thread.

Your tatting lace table runner is now ready to adorn your dining table with elegance and style!

Tatting Lace Cuff Bracelet

Materials Needed:

- Tatting needle
- Tatting thread
- Cuff bracelet base (metal or fabric)
- Fabric glue or needle and thread
- Scissors

Instructions:

Tat a series of lace motifs, such as flowers, leaves, or geometric shapes, using a combination of rings, chains, and picots.

Once the motifs are complete, Cut off any extra thread and firmly secure the ends.

Attach the tatting lace motifs to a cuff bracelet base using fabric glue or by stitching them in place with needle and thread.

Allow the glue to dry completely or finish securing the motifs with additional stitching.

Optionally, embellish the cuff bracelet with beads, sequins, or charms for extra sparkle and flair.

Your tatting lace cuff bracelet is now ready to wear as a stylish and eye-catching accessory!

Tatting Lace Wall Hanging

Materials Needed:

- Tatting needle
- Tatting thread
- Wooden dowel or branch for hanging
- Yarn or string for hanging
- Fabric glue or needle and thread
- Scissors

Instructions:

Tat a series of lace motifs, edging, or panels using advanced tatting techniques and patterns.

Once the tatting is complete, Cut off any extra thread and firmly secure the ends.

Attach the tatting to a wooden dowel or branch for hanging using fabric glue or by stitching it in place with needle and thread.

Cut a length of yarn or string and attach it to the ends of the wooden dowel or branch to create a hanger for the wall hanging.

Optionally, add beads, feathers, or other embellishments to the wall hanging for extra texture and visual interest.

Your tatting lace wall hanging is now ready to adorn your walls with elegance and charm!

Tatting Lace Wedding Garter

Materials Needed:

- Tatting needle
- Tatting thread
- Elastic lace or ribbon for garter base
- Fabric glue or needle and thread
- Scissors
- Beads, sequins, or charms for embellishment (optional)

Instructions:

Tat a series of intricate lace motifs or edging using advanced tatting techniques.

Once the tatting is complete, Cut off any extra thread and firmly secure the ends.

Attach the tatting lace to an elastic lace or ribbon garter base using fabric glue or by stitching it in place with needle and thread.

Optionally, embellish the garter with beads, sequins, or charms for added sparkle and detail.

Your tatting lace wedding garter is now ready to be worn as a beautiful and meaningful accessory on your special day!

Tatting Lace Book Cover

Materials Needed:

- Tatting needle
- Tatting thread
- Fabric for book cover base
- Cardboard or chipboard for book cover reinforcement (optional)
- Fabric glue or needle and thread
- Scissors
- Button or ribbon for closure (optional)
- Decorative elements such as beads or charms (optional)

Instructions:

Tat a series of lace motifs or panels using advanced tatting techniques to create the desired design for your book cover.

Once the tatting is complete, Cut off any extra thread and firmly secure the ends.

Prepare the fabric for the book cover base by cutting it to the desired size and shape, and if desired, reinforce it with cardboard or chipboard.

Attach the tatting lace to the fabric base using fabric glue or by stitching it in place with needle and thread.

Optionally, add a button or ribbon closure to the book cover for a decorative touch and practical function.

Embellish the book cover with additional decorative elements such as beads or charms for extra detail and flair.

Your tatting lace book cover is now ready to protect and adorn your favorite books with elegance and style!

CHAPTER 6

Troubleshooting

Troubleshooting needle tatting can sometimes be a bit challenging, but here are some common issues and their potential solutions:

Knots or Tangles:

Issue: Your thread keeps getting tangled or forming knots while tatting.

Solution: Ensure that your working area is well organized and that your thread has enough slack to move freely. Avoid pulling the thread too tightly after each stitch, as this can cause knots to form. Take breaks to untangle the thread if necessary, and consider using a thread conditioner to reduce friction and prevent tangling.

Uneven Stitches:

Issue: Your tatting stitches are uneven in size or tension, resulting in an irregular appearance.

Solution: Practice consistent tension control by holding the needle and thread in a relaxed grip. Make sure to pull the thread snugly after each stitch to create even tension. Pay attention to the size of your picots and double stitches (ds) to ensure uniformity throughout your tatting project. With practice, your stitches will become more consistent over time.

Difficulty Reading Patterns:

Issue: You're having trouble understanding or following tatting patterns.

Solution: Take your time to carefully read through the pattern instructions, paying attention to any abbreviations or symbols used. Break down the pattern into smaller sections and practice each part individually before attempting the entire project. Don't hesitate to reach out to online tatting communities or forums for clarification if you encounter any difficulties.

Rings or Chains Not Closing Properly:

Issue: Your rings or chains are not closing properly, resulting in gaps or loops in your tatting.

Solution: Ensure that you are making each stitch snugly and evenly, without leaving too much slack in the thread. Double-check that you are following the pattern instructions correctly, including the number of double stitches (ds) and picots required for each element. If necessary, gently manipulate the stitches with your needle to adjust their positioning and close any gaps.

Thread Breakage:

Issue: Your thread keeps breaking while tatting, causing frustration and interruptions.

Solution: Use high-quality tatting thread that is strong and durable. Avoid using old or worn-out thread that may be prone to breaking. Check your needle periodically for any burrs or rough edges that could be damaging the thread, and replace it if necessary. If your thread does break, carefully rejoin it using a secure knot or splice to minimize disruptions to your tatting project.

General Tips

Start with the Basics: Begin with simple projects and basic techniques to familiarize yourself with the fundamentals of needle tatting. Practice forming double stitches (ds), picots, rings, and chains until you feel comfortable with the movements and rhythm.

Use Quality Materials: Invest in high-quality tatting needles and thread for smoother and more enjoyable tatting sessions. Choose threads that are specifically designed for tatting, such as cotton or silk, in a size appropriate for your chosen project.

Maintain Even Tension: Consistent tension is key to achieving uniform stitches and a professional-looking finish. Practice maintaining an even tension throughout your tatting work by holding the needle and thread in a relaxed grip and pulling the thread snugly after each stitch.

Take Breaks: Tatting can be intricate and time-consuming, so don't forget to take breaks to rest your hands and eyes. Stretching your fingers and wrists periodically can help prevent fatigue and discomfort during longer tatting sessions.

Practice Patience: Needle tatting requires patience and practice to master, so don't be discouraged by mistakes or setbacks. Embrace the learning process and celebrate your progress with each project you complete.

Reference Resources: Keep tatting books, tutorials, and patterns on hand for inspiration and guidance. Online resources, such as video tutorials and forums, can also be valuable sources of information and support for beginner and experienced tatters alike.

Experiment and Innovate: Don't be afraid to experiment with different techniques, thread colors, and embellishments to customize your tatting projects and make them uniquely your own. Innovation and creativity are integral parts of the tatting process.

Practice Mindfulness: Tatting can be a meditative and relaxing activity that allows you to focus your mind and unwind from the stresses of daily life. Practice mindfulness while tatting by paying attention to the sensations of the thread and needle in your hands, as well as the rhythmic movements of the stitches.

Celebrate Your Achievements: Each completed tatting project is a testament to your creativity, skill, and dedication. Take pride in your accomplishments and celebrate the beauty of handmade lace that you've created with your own two hands.

CONCLUSION

Needle tatting is a beautiful and versatile craft that offers endless possibilities for creativity and expression. From delicate lace accessories to intricate home decor items, tatting allows enthusiasts to create handmade treasures that are both timeless and unique.

Throughout this book, we've explored the history and origins of needle tatting, delved into the benefits and versatility of this craft, discussed essential tools and materials, and provided step-by-step instructions for mastering basic and advanced techniques. We've also shared a variety of beginner, intermediate, and advanced projects to inspire your tatting journey and help you develop your skills.

Whether you're a beginner just starting out or an experienced tatter looking to expand your repertoire, there's always something new to learn and explore in the world of needle tatting. By practicing patience, embracing creativity, and enjoying the process, you can create beautiful tatting pieces that bring joy to yourself and others.

As you continue on your tatting journey, remember to celebrate your achievements, share your knowledge with fellow enthusiasts, and above all, have fun with your craft. Whether you're tatting for relaxation, self-expression, or to create handmade gifts for loved ones, the satisfaction of creating something beautiful with your own two hands is truly incomparable. Happy tatting!

Made in the USA
Las Vegas, NV
31 May 2025